I Know Someone with
Allergies

Vic Parker

www.raintreepublishers.co.uk
Visit our website to find out
more information about
Raintree books.

To order:
☎ Phone 0845 6044371
🖷 Fax +44 (0) 1865 312263
🖳 Email myorders@raintreepublishers.co.uk

Customers from outside the UK please telephone +44 1865 312262

Raintree is an imprint of Capstone Global Library
Limited, a company incorporated in England and
Wales having its registered office at 7 Pilgrim Street,
London, EC4V 6LB – Registered company number:
6695582

Text © Capstone Global Library Limited 2011
First published in hardback in 2011
The moral rights of the proprietor have been asserted.

Edited by Rebecca Rissman, Daniel Nunn
   and Siân Smith
Designed by Joanna Hinton Malivoire
Picture research by Mica Brancic
Originated by Capstone Global Library
Printed and bound in China by Leo Paper Products Ltd

ISBN 978 1 406 22072 8
15 14 13 12 11
10 9 8 7 6 5 4 3 2 1

British Library Cataloguing in Publication Data
Parker, Victoria.
I know someone with allergies. – (Understanding
health issues)
   1. Allergy–Juvenile literature.
   I. Title II. Series

616.9'7-dc22

Acknowledgements
We would like to thank the following for permission to
reproduce photographs: Alamy pp. 6 (© Purestock/
Steve Smith), 7 (© Bubbles Photolibrary), 15 (© Kari
Marttila); Corbis pp. 4 (© cultura), 14 (© Image
Source); Getty pp. 17 (Blend Images/Granger Wootz),
18 (Photodisc/Matthias Tunger), 22 (Brand X Pictures/
Sarah M. Golonka), 23 (Science Photo Library/Ian
Adene), 25 (Getty Images Sport/Clive Brunskill); Getty
Images News p. 24 (Bongarts/Friedemann Vogel);
iStockphoto pp. 10 (© Jill Chen), 13 (© Grzegorz Kula),
16 (© Tomaz Levstek), 20 (© Monika Adamczyk);
Photolibrary p. 26 (Fotosearch value); Science Photo
Library pp. 5 (Ian Boddy), 11 (Edwige), 21 (Coneyl Jay);
Shutterstock pp. 12 (© Blaj Gabriel), 19 (© Quayside),
27 (© Paulaphoto).

Cover photograph of a woman sneezing reproduced
with permission of Getty Images (Cultura/Colin
Hawkins).

We would like to thank Matthew Siegel and Ashley
Wolinski for their invaluable help in the preparation of
this book.

Every effort has been made to contact copyright
holders of any material reproduced in this book. Any
omissions will be rectified in subsequent printings if
notice is given to the publisher.

All the Internet addresses (URLs) given in this book
were valid at the time of going to press. However, due
to the dynamic nature of the Internet, some addresses
may have changed, or sites may have changed or
ceased to exist since publication. While the author and
publisher regret any inconvenience this may cause
readers, no responsibility for any such changes can be
accepted by either the author or the publisher.

Contents

Some words are printed in bold, **like this**. You can find out what they mean in the glossary.

Do you know someone with allergies?

You might have a friend with an allergy. This means that something which doesn't usually harm people has a bad effect on their body.

Cat hair can make an allergic person's eyes itch, swell, go red, and water.

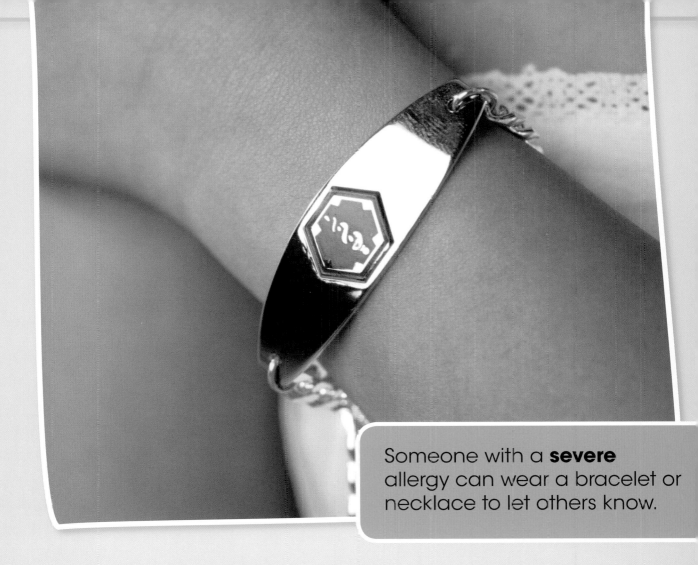

Someone with a **severe** allergy can wear a bracelet or necklace to let others know.

You cannot usually tell that someone has allergies by looking at them. A person's body only shows allergies when they are around the things they are allergic to. We call these things **allergens**.

What is an allergic reaction?

Our bodies try to fight off harmful things, such as colds and coughs, by making special chemicals inside us called **antibodies**.

Some harmful **infections** can make you sneeze.

When someone meets something they are allergic to, their body thinks it is harmful and makes antibodies to fight it. These build up, causing bad effects. This is an **allergic reaction**.

What can people be allergic to?

There are lots of things people can be allergic to. Some of these things are shown in the table below.

Allergens you can touch or that can touch you	• rubber • grass • pet hair • washing powder • bee/wasp/hornet stings
Allergens you can breathe in	• dust • plant **pollen** • moulds • perfume • cigarette smoke
Allergens you can swallow	• medicine • milk • fish • strawberries • sesame seeds

Allergens can affect people in different ways. Someone with a strong peanut allergy might become ill through eating a peanut, or by touching one. They could even become ill just by breathing in tiny pieces of peanut.

STOP!
nut
free
zone

please do not bring
nuts into this area

You can help children who are allergic to nuts by not taking things with nuts in to school.

Who has allergies?

Anyone can develop allergies at any time. Nobody knows why some people get certain allergies. However, some allergies, like peanut allergy, are becoming more common.

Allergies seem to run in families.

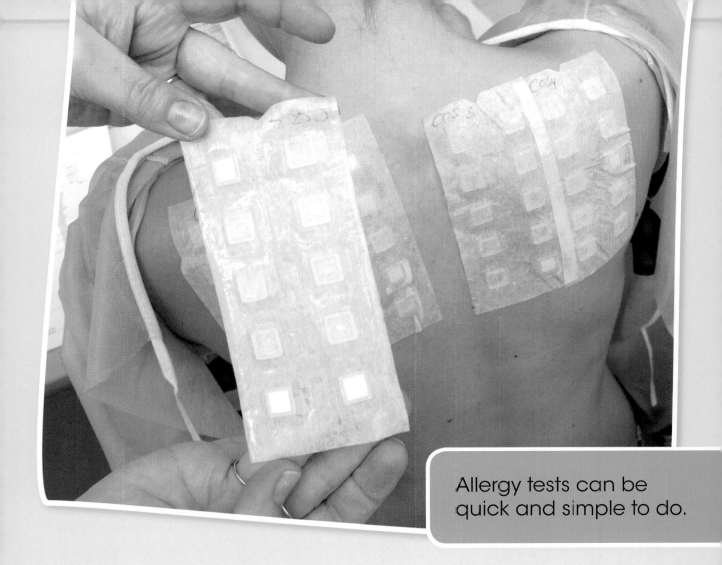

Allergy tests can be quick and simple to do.

It is usually simple for a doctor or nurse to find out if someone is allergic to something. There are easy tests they can do on someone's blood or skin.

Living with allergies

People can have allergens as injections, tablets, or drops under their tongue.

A doctor can try to **cure** someone of an allergy by giving them lots of very tiny amounts of the **allergen**. But this only works in some cases. No one knows why.

For most people, the only way to deal with their allergies is to keep away from the things that they are allergic to. Then they will not have **allergic reactions**.

You can help a friend with an allergy to **pollen** by playing indoors when the **pollen count** is high.

Avoiding allergens

For many people, it can be hard to avoid **allergens**. For instance, dust and grass are often all around us. People can be bothered by these sorts of allergies a lot of the time.

Allergies can be constantly irritating.

This boy has had an allergic reaction to a hornet sting.

Other people may have **allergic reactions** very rarely, such as when they are stung by a bee or a hornet. But these reactions can be **severe**. Such people may feel worried, or even frightened, now and again.

Helping hay fever sufferers

Someone who is allergic to grass and **pollen** might have a difficult time during spring and summer. They may have puffy, itchy eyes and a blocked or runny nose. This type of **allergic reaction** to the outdoors is called hay fever.

Many plants make pollen in spring and summer. This can cause problems for people with hay fever.

People with hay fever do not have to miss out on outdoor fun if they take allergy medicine.

People with hay fever can take medicines to help their eyes and nose get better. Some of these are tablets or liquid to swallow. There are also eye and nose drops, and sprays to squirt up the nose.

Soothing skin

Someone allergic to horse hair may react with hives.

Someone may have an **allergic reaction** to something on their skin, either in one place or all over. Hives is an itchy skin rash caused by **allergens**.

Medicines can make allergic skin reactions less itchy. Some of these are tablets or liquid you swallow. Other medicines include creams that you rub in.

Eczema is a reaction that makes skin itchy, but using special creams for eczema can help a lot.

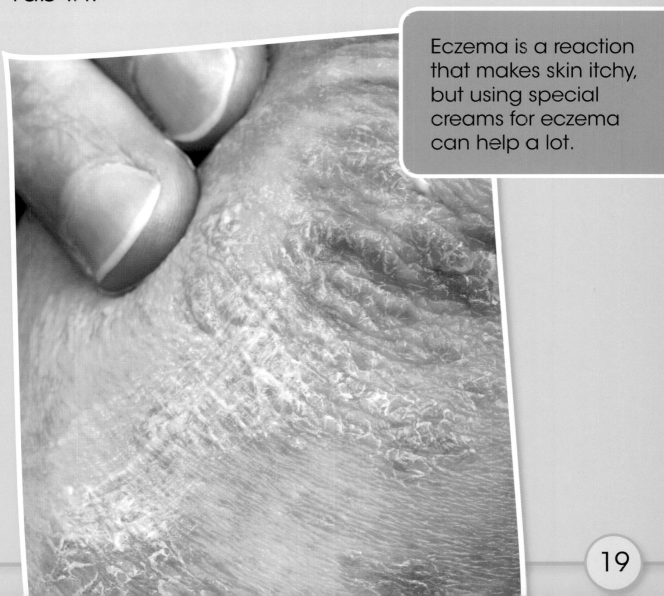

Opening airways

Someone having an **allergic reaction** may become **wheezy** and short of breath. This happens when the airways inside their body suddenly narrow, so they cannot get enough air.

Someone might become short of breath because of an allergy to house dust.

If a friend with allergic asthma becomes short of breath you can help by telling a grown-up.

This type of reaction is called allergic asthma. If you have a friend with allergic asthma they may take medicine that helps them through a special spray called an **inhaler**.

Emergency!

In a **severe allergic reaction**, a person's whole body develops a rash and swells. Their mouth and throat can become so swollen that airways get blocked, so the person cannot breathe. This happens extremely fast.

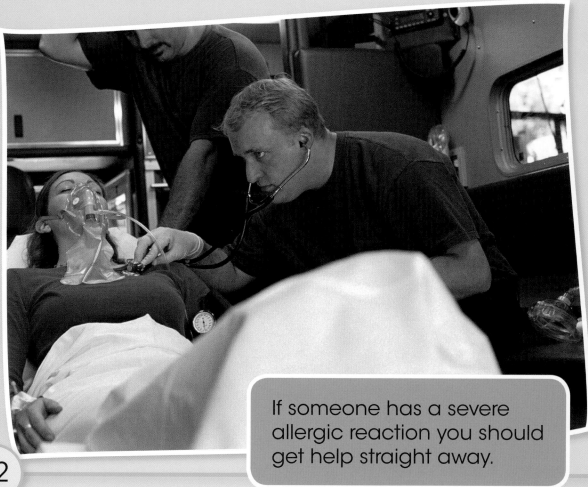

If someone has a severe allergic reaction you should get help straight away.

An injection can help someone with a severe allergic reaction, until they reach hospital.

Severe allergic reactions usually happen to people who are allergic to certain foods, such as eggs. These people should always carry a special injection with them that can stop the reaction for a while.

Famous people

Lleyton Hewitt is an Australian tennis player who suffers from an allergy to grass. However, this has not stopped him winning tennis tournaments played on grass, such as Queens and Wimbledon.

Lleyton Hewitt has shown that allergies don't have to stop you doing what you want to do.

Serena Williams is one of the world's greatest female tennis players.

Tennis superstar Serena Williams is allergic to peanuts. She is extremely fit and healthy and has won Wimbledon several times.

Being a good friend

There are many ways you can be a good friend to someone with allergies. For example, you can remove anything they might be allergic to before they come to visit you.

If someone who is allergic to pet hair comes to visit, you can help by moving pets out of the room and vacuuming up any hair.

We all have different bodies and different personalities.

Living with allergies can be difficult at times. We are all different in many ways. A good friend likes us and values us for who we are.

Allergies – facts and fiction

Facts

- For every five people around the world one is likely to have an allergy.

- Someone can get an allergy at any time in their life.

- People can be allergic to more than one thing.

Fiction

(?) People with hay fever can avoid **pollen** by heading to the seaside.

WRONG! Pollen can travel for many kilometres on the wind, even out to sea.

(?) You can catch allergies from other people.

WRONG! You cannot catch an allergy from someone else.

(?) You cannot grow out of allergies.

WRONG! You can grow out of some allergies.

Glossary

allergen something which can cause harm to someone's body, although it is not harmful to most people

allergic reaction in an allergic reaction someone's body reacts badly to something they touch, breathe, eat, or drink

antibodies our bodies make antibodies in our blood to fight off germs and keep us well

cure medical treatment that makes someone better

infection illness caused by germs

inhaler small piece of equipment you use to breathe in certain medicines

pollen fine powder made by certain plants

pollen count measurement of the amount of pollen in the air

severe extremely bad

wheezy if someone is wheezy, they make a high, rough noise when they breathe because they are having difficulty breathing

Find out more

Books to read

Allergies (How's Your Health?), Angela Royston (Franklin Watts 2010)

Allergies (It's not catching), Angela Royston (Heinemann Library, 2004)

Aneil has a food allergy (Like Me, Like You), Jillian Powell (Evans Brothers 2009)

Websites

kidshealth.org/kid/asthma_basics/related/allergies.html

Find out more about allergies on this website.

kidshealth.org/teen/your_mind/friends/helping_allergies.html

This website tells you all about food allergies.

Index